# Small Business Survival in the 21st Century
## *Some Pearls of Wisdom - Believe It or Not!*

### by- Dr. MAXWELL S. PINTO

ISBN: **978-0-9877504-5-7**

Published by Maxwell S.C. Pinto 978-0-9877504-5-7
Copyright 2012 Maxwell S. C. Pinto
This book is licensed for your personal enjoyment only. This book may not be re-sold or given away to other people. If you would like to share this book with another person, please purchase an additional copy for each recipient.

*During the preparation of this book, several books were reviewed and lost due to an unfortunate incident. I thank the publishers and authors of those books and sources that I accessed on the Internet and I apologize for not being able to include their names in the bibliography section of this book.- Dr. Maxwell S. Pinto*

### Dedication

This is my sixth book on leadership and business management. This book is dedicated to my family and friends, who have always encouraged me to write books on the subject of ethical leadership and management in the 21st century. Hopefully, this book will benefit students, lay people, businesspersons and professionals alike.

# About the Author

Dr. Maxwell S. Pinto is an established business consultant and author, with several professional credentials, including a PhD in business administration from Pacific Southern University, California, and the Chartered Accountant's designation from England and Wales. He is also a Life Member of the Institute of Professional Managers and Administrators (UK).

Dr. Pinto is fluent in several languages, with international experience in Profitability Analysis, Corporate Restructuring, Management Information Systems, Training and Development, and other areas of business. Dr. Pinto conducts seminars and engages in radio interviews on leadership, ethics, workplace bullying and women in the workforce. This book is a follow up to his highly acclaimed and authoritative manuals on leadership: 'The Management Syndrome: How to Deal with It!', 'Leadership: Flirting with Disaster!', 'Management: *Tidbits for the New Millennium!*', 'Leadership and Ethics: Major Ingredients of the Business Recipe' and "Ethical Leadership: Fact or Fiction?" Dr. Pinto has a specific commitment towards working with business persons, in a bottom line approach to solving their problems. Instead of focusing on mere numbers, leaders should understand that people matter and that their recruitment, training and motivation within an ethical team environment will affect the bottom line.

# PREFACE

This is my sixth book on leadership and business management. This book is meant to provide easy reading for those interested in grasping the essentials of business survival, with emphasis on ethical leadership in the real world. This guide covers Leadership, Customer Service, Negotiation, Home-based Business Organizations, Trade Unions, Japanese Management, Women in the Workforce, Financial Controls, Motivation and other areas of business, in a nutshell. The earlier editions of this book were reviewed by businessmen, professionals, students and others. This edition is based on their feedback and review.

## Acknowledgements

I am indebted to Maurice Pinto; Mark Pinto, M.B.A.,Ch.FC.; Krishna Prasad, BSc.; Aley Thomas, M.B.A.; Eusebia Menezes-Pinto, M.A.; M.Sc., Maurice Coutinho, VP, American Express, Josie Gelacio, B.Ed.; Mari-jane Sutton; Aaron Pinto, M.Sc.; Esther Pinto and others, whose names I may have overlooked, but to whom I am eternally grateful.

# CONTENTS

1    Leadership in the 21st Century: Some Pearls of Wisdom

    Believe It or Not

    Is "Ethical Leadership" an Oxymoron?

    Customers – Are they Always Right?

    Efficiency versus Effectiveness

    Knowledge and Implementation

    Nervousness - Does it Help?

    Negotiation - A Game?

    Uniqueness

    Teams: Functional or Dysfunctional?

    Is it Best to be Your Own Boss?

    The Business Plan - An Important Blueprint?

    Operations, Technology and Other Matters

    Acquiring an Existing Business?

    The Importance of a Good Lawyer, Accountant and Others

    Communication, Business Dealings and Interpersonal Relations

2. Financial and Other Matters: Some Pearls of Wisdom

>Does Cost-cutting Improve the Bottom Line?
>
>Does Technical Efficiency Enable Managerial Efficiency?
>
>No One is Indispensable!
>
>The Role of Women in the Workplace and at Home
>
>Japanese Managers - Too Slow in Decision Making?
>
>Trade Unions - Are They Evil?

3. The Law, Ethics and Other Matters: Some Pearls of Wisdom

>The Law
>
>The Law of Contract
>
>Mistake
>
>Misrepresentation
>
>Discharge of Contract
>
>Remedies for Breach of Contract
>
>Other Matters Relating to Contracts
>
>The Nature of Contract
>
>Signatures on the Contract
>
>Signed and Sealed
>
>Hard Copies and Electronic Copies
>
>E-mail Contracts
>
>Contract Modification
>
>Choice of Law and Choice of Jurisdiction
>
>Contracts for the International Sale of Goods 1980 (CISG)
>
>The Statute of Frauds
>
>Analysis of the Substance of the Contract

Agency

Relationship between Agent and Principal

Ethics

Anger Management

**Ethics, Legal Implications and Reputation**

Conclusion

4. Some Final Thoughts on Leadership

Humor

Change and the Ability to Manage Change

Telecommuting

Workplace Bullying

Undergraduates Seeking Work Experience

Teamwork

Motivation

Communication

Training

Meetings

Drucker's View: The Corporation— A SymphonyOrchestra

Where Do We Go From Here?

5. BIBLIOGRAPHY

# CHAPTER 1 – Leadership in the 21st Century: *Some Pearls of Wisdom*

**Believe It or Not**

1. Leadership is about vision, teamwork, opportunities and appropriate action and the term "business ethics" is often regarded as an oxymoron!

2. The Internet has greatly impacted the way we communicate with one another and this sometimes has an adverse impact on human relations, in the sense that people who could be talking to one another prefer to send e-mail messages to one another!

Leadership is the art of mobilizing others toward shared aspirations while taking care of ***all*** stakeholders: owners, managers, other employees, customers, suppliers, the government, the community, etc., *rather than the customer alone*, in order to promote *overall* welfare. Great leaders are visionaries whose intuition and teamwork enable them to capitalize on business opportunities. They surround themselves with "like-minded" professionals who complement them to reinforce their strengths, eliminate their weaknesses and improve their bottom line. They realize that profits result from fruitful relationships and they are willing to distribute some of these profits in a fair manner, in the sincere belief that this will promote overall welfare. They believe in sharing the existing pie and motivating others to increase its size, rather than in selfishly retaining the largest possible share of the existing pie, and in so doing, reducing its size as a result of demotivation of employees and other stakeholders.

Great leaders lead by (ethical) example: morals, fairness, caring, sharing, no false promises or unreasonable demands on others, etc., and structure compensation packages which promote effectiveness.

**Is "Ethical Leadership" an Oxymoron?**

Well, this would depend on how you review the term "business ethics." There are those who insist that the term "happily married" is an oxymoron, in the sense that marriage contributes to a compromise of one's freedom and increased stress levels. There are others who will confirm that the synergistic effects of marriage more than outweigh the results of the compromise involved. When it comes to business ethics, it is extremely difficult to comply at all times because we do not have all the answers. For instance, when dealing with a prospect, should the salesperson disclose all material facts regarding the product or service in question (and that of the competition) or is it the buyer's responsibility to conduct due diligence? Should the salesperson answer each question exactly as it was asked, and ignore some pertinent information or should he or she merely address the spirit of the question?

In order to operate effectively within a human environment one must understand what makes people tick and what upsets them, while bearing in mind that no two individuals are alike. In other words, if you approach somebody who is time-conscious, make sure you are on time and precise, otherwise you will not achieve the desired result. Also bear in mind that some people are more conscious about their status and the ethical nature of the company they work for than about their salaries. Such individuals refuse to work for a company which encourages a toxic culture. The saying "Money talks" does not apply to them.

**Efficiency versus Effectiveness**

Peter Drucker, the guru of management thinkers, drew our attention to the difference between efficiency and effectiveness. Drucker claimed that efficiency involved "doing things right" whereas effectiveness involved "doing the right things right," i.e. prioritizing and operating accordingly.

Managers should motivate their employees through respect, teamwork and sharing, training, increased responsibility, challenging assignments, open book management and participative management. If leaders treat employees like family and show them that they care for them, they will reap rewards in terms of loyalty and bottom-line oriented performance. Instead of being short-sighted and focusing only on short-term gains, leaders should focus on profitable growth in the short, medium and long terms.

Leaders should be speedy in approach with stakeholders and outsiders or face the consequences of being left behind. "Slow and steady wins the race" is a formula for mediocrity! Although speed is of the essence, quality must never be compromised. The lead time between the awareness of a problem and its solution should be as short as possible, bearing in mind Drucker's emphasis on effectiveness, as discussed earlier.

**Customers – Are they Always Right?**

Developing a relationship with customers is based on trust, results and adaptation to their changing needs. Listen carefully to your customers, understand their needs and try to satisfy them, bearing in mind that the customer is *not* always right, i.e., you should not make other stakeholders suffer unduly at the expense of the customer.

**Knowledge and Implementation**

No given individual can claim to know everything relating to his or her role in the organization. Therefore, it is virtuous to admit shortcomings and to work towards eliminating them. Individuals should be open to the possibility of continuous learning, while being aware that good ideas are useless unless they are followed up through implementation, in a timely manner. Good ideas should be shared with others, many of whom will return the favour at an opportune time.

Decision making should be effected on the basis of comprehensive information which is relevant, accurate and timely, experience and intuition, rather than logic alone. To assume that people adopt a rational approach to decision making is to be naïve, because intuition does play a significant role in a world of uncertainty. Decision making should be preceded by careful thought and due consideration. That being said, bad decisions should be reversed e.g. firing an employee who was hired for the wrong reason and who can no longer perform in line with the required standards, despite the organization's best efforts to keep the employee on track.

**Nervousness - Does it Help?**

A certain amount of nervousness helps conscientious people work harder to achieve their goals, be it in business, personal life, sports or any other field. Therefore, if you are completely relaxed, there is a distinct possibility that there is something wrong—perhaps you are under-estimating the task at hand, as when Nastase played Borg at Wimbledon in 1976. On the other hand, if one is too nervous, the same result can be expected, as when Andy Murray played Roger Federer at the Australian Open in 2010.

**Negotiation - A Game?**

In a game one party wins. In a negotiation, a win-win situation for all parties involved is of utmost importance; otherwise the business relationship will be short-lived. As Mahatma Gandhi once said "...there is enough (in this world) for everyone's need, but not for everyone's greed." An ethical approach to business takes this into account and contributes to profitable growth.

We should always be fair in our dealings with others. Treat others as you would have them treat you and you will be blessed in business and personal life, not only in terms of money, but also in terms of inner satisfaction, which is difficult to quantify in monetary terms. In any relationship, it is important for both parties to realize their responsibilities and opportunities.

**Uniqueness**

Individuals are unique, each with his or her own talents, which should be recognized, respected and rewarded. People who are intelligent in terms of logic may be lacking in terms of emotional intelligence. People should be assigned with responsibilities on the basis of their skills, their flexibility and their ability to operate as members of the team in question.

**Teams: Functional or Dysfunctional?**

Teams should be formed on the basis of the required tasks and should consist of members who complement one another in terms of skills, personalities and other variables. The importance of ethical solutions should always be stressed. Principles should never be compromised. Profitable growth is usually the goal, though not at the expense of one's principles being compromised, otherwise the organization will be regarded as lacking in character, success may be short-lived and eventually wiped out by lawsuits and damages.
In order for a team to be effective there should be trust among team members and this may need to be built up over a period of time, through shared experiences, discussions and bonding.

Communication and feedback are extremely important. Healthy conflict, e.g., via discussions or debates should be encouraged rather than feared and eliminated. Team members should be committed and held accountable for team goals and their achievement, for their attitudes, as well as for their acts and omissions.

**Is it Best to be Your Own Boss?**

Bad bosses are guilty of workplace bullying tactics which adversely affect the financial and emotional health of employees and result in high employee turnover, with associated costs to business organizations and the families of the targets, victims and witnesses of bullying. Very often the bullies are supervisors and managers against whom human resource departments are reluctant to act for fear of the repercussions. In some cases, legal or other actions follow and result in unnecessary costs for the organization that entertains bullying. *Every person who leaves a corporation becomes its ambassador, for better or for worse!*

Employees usually feel the need to be motivated via ethical leadership: respect, caring, sharing, challenging assignments, etc., a reasonable compensation package, combined with praise, fair criticism, challenging assignments, participative management and by other methods. The failure on the part of leaders to motivate employees often encourages employees to start off on their own. But frustration with one's boss does not justify starting off on one's own, unless one has the required knowledge, discipline and support system to operate one's own business, whether from one's own home or elsewhere. One needs to be able to "roll with the punches" when things do not go according to plan. There are times when you will have to work alone, without anyone to talk to or liaise with. Spare time must be used constructively.

Technical expertise, though advantageous, does not guarantee business success! Many business organizations close down in the early years, thus confirming the need for (ethical) leadership and marketing skills, in addition to technical skills and adequate cash flow. Prior to starting off on one's own, one should attend courses which relate to the leadership, managerial and planning aspects of business. In addition, one has to learn from the mistakes of one's former supervisors and managers and treat employees as precious investments, in an ethical manner. This will ensure their loyalty while contributing to personal, as well as (profitable) corporate growth. A home based business may be geared towards providing supplemental income, replacing one's full time job or an attempt to supplement retirement income. An action plan based on marketable skills must be accompanied by a willingness to put in a concerted effort, aimed at achieving one's goals within a reasonable period of time, with profit and cash flow in mind.

Setting up your home based business will have implications for your family life. Therefore, communicate with your family and ensure that you spend quality time with them, giving them their space, adequate telephone usage, confidentiality regarding the presence of family, friends, neighbors, disturbances and so on. All family members and friends should understand that there are certain sacrifices which may have to be made, at least until the business is considered to be operating at the desired level, given the time frame and other constraints involved. Establish a healthy relationship with a bank which is known for good service. Ensure that the appropriate licenses are in place to enable you to operate legally and efficiently. You may wish to have a logo which identifies your business and promotes effective advertising.

**The Business Plan - An Important Blueprint?**

A business plan does help provide a blueprint for success and can be adjusted, if necessary. A business plan outlines the history of the business, its nature and purpose, short-, medium- and long-term goals, the target market and characteristics, market research conducted, competitive strategy and related matters. The business plan must include financial statements to show where the business is headed over the next (say) three years, based on expectations.

**Operations, Technology and Other Matters**

Be aware of your situation and set up your office accordingly, bearing in mind space requirements, storage, number and frequency of customers, neat appearance of the office and surrounding area, lighting, the floor, furniture, feng shui, hygiene factors, cleaning, mail services, filing, bookshelves, zoning, parking, entrance, greeting customers and related factors.

As far as technology is concerned, ensure that you have good quality telephones, an efficient computer with suitable software and easy access to the Internet in a speedy manner. Technology and work of a high quality must be complemented by excellent customer service.

**Acquiring an Existing Business?**

If you are considering buying a business, review the financial statements for the past few years, and the credibility of the accountant and take into account location, market share, growth rate, assets, liabilities and undisclosed items, such as obsolete inventories or inventories held but not paid for, unless it can be proved that the responsibility for payment rests with the current owner. Also consider pending lawsuits, possible goodwill and ensure that the agreement of sale prevents the current owner from competing with you for a certain specified period of time and within a certain radius of your location. Also interview existing employees and discuss your acquisition plans with them. Distribute questionnaires to ascertain what current employees like and dislike about the company which you are hoping to acquire.

**The Importance of a Good Lawyer, Accountant and Others**

A business organization needs a good lawyer, a good accountant, a good insurance company and a good banking relationship, for obvious reasons. Liability insurance, workers' compensation, business interruption insurance, health, dental, medical and disability insurance, property insurance, auto insurance and related matters should also be taken into consideration.

**Communication, Business Dealings and Interpersonal Relations**

You must stay organized and communicate well with stakeholders and others. Be careful in your dealings with people and also note that you will be busier at certain times of the day. Communication face to face, over the phone, via e-mail messages and letters should be courteous and effective. Pay yourself reasonably for the services you provide - *you are not working free for your own business!*

Stay focused and motivated, be creative, attend training courses and business events, join volunteer organizations and look for lines of business which complement your own line of business. Promote yourself at all times, whether you are attending a function or merely visiting a mall, but do not appear to be desperate for new business. Your communication skills and style of operation must impress people, so that they want to do business with you. Advertising helps, but it must be complemented by excellent service and follow-up. *People are attracted to successful businessmen, rather than businessmen who are depressed and needy – always bear this in mind.*

When you are unproven and starting a business or changing careers, working for free or offering one free service or session, is an effective way of gaining experience and developing fruitful business relationships.

# CHAPTER 2 – Financial and Other Matters: *Some Pearls of Wisdom*

Many leaders hesitate to invest money on projects whose outcomes are uncertain. They often tend to be cost conscious with realizing the possible impact of motivation. They do not like to entertain the thought of "nothing venture, nothing gain."

**Does Cost-cutting Improve the Bottom Line?**

Cost cutting does not necessarily improve the bottom line. For instance, if the quality of materials acquired for production is compromised, there will be an adverse effect on labor costs and materials damaged during production. Moreover, customers may be displeased with the final product and customer service costs will rise accordingly. Also, if salaries are reduced productivity may fall due to the de-motivational impact on employees.

**Does Technical Efficiency Enable Managerial Efficiency?**

Many managers in the corporate world possess technical ability without adequate managerial expertise and are therefore unable to motivate employees sufficiently in line with corporate goals, largely because these managers do not possess the right skill set. Managers by occupation (rather than by profession) usually adermine the importance of ethical leadership, teamwork, motivation, preparation and development, feedback, communication, interpersonal skills, tact, and other factors. These individuals cost the business organization far more than the salaries they are paid, but they continue to be employed and promoted without even being tested for adequate managerial skills—this confirms the application of "The Peter Principle." The proper balance must be struck between technical and managerial skills otherwise the bottom line will suffer.

**No One is Indispensable!**

It is true that no one is indispensable. It is also true that we need effective teamwork to improve the bottom line. This being the case we need employees to be selected on the basis of merit and motivated via an ethical approach and goal congruence. This will also avoid costs associated with high employee turnover, which results mainly from poor management skills.

## The Role of Women in the Workplace and at Home

Men and women should operate as a team, with synergy in mind, instead of being threatened by the presence or performance of members of the opposite gender. What we need is a positive approach to life and business in an attempt to increase personal, corporate, national, and international welfare.

The social, cultural, and political attitudes of modern society have enabled women to seize power from men, despite being treated unfairly by unethical leaders, who continue to reinforce the (bullet-proof) "glass ceiling" instead of shattering it, and despite having to leave the workforce due to family considerations, and then return a few years later, in some cases. Women understand that fruitful conversations promote sound business relationships and teamwork, thus contributing to an improvement in the bottom line.

Women are usually well organized: they manage a dual career, as homemakers and professional employees. Women often regard their fellow employees as family and take time to ascertain their personal needs. Hence, they can sometimes be taken undue advantage of. Competition is strange to most women because they were groomed for caring, rather than winning! A former Mayor of Ottawa once said, "Whatever women do, they must do twice as well as men to be thought of as half as good. Luckily, this is not difficult!"

When women become intoxicated by power, they lose their identity and bearings. Women should focus on a diplomatic approach and learn how to exude self-confidence while maintaining self-respect and dealing with the competition without being intimidated or taken undue advantage of. Women who achieve powerful positions in the corporate world may be subjected to personal and professional attacks because of their gender. Independent women are strong, fearless, and in control of their homes, families, emotions, and their working environment. They tackle problems with a heads-on approach, being steadfast in their pursuit of success and happiness.


## Japanese Managers - Too Slow in Decision Making?

The Japanese are known for thoroughly analyzing the nature and extent of problems and adopting a systematic approach to decision-making, which involves the following:
- Defining the problem precisely and reaching a consensus about the definition of the problems—the action stage;
- Entrusting the problem to the appropriate group, selected by top management, for a detailed effective solution; and
- Implementing their decision and obtaining feedback.

*Defining the problem*: The Japanese decision-making system is called the *Ringi*, where harmony is the key value and decision-making is by *group* consensus upon careful diagnosis of the problem. The Japanese believe that in order to find the best solution to a problem, there must be imagination, creativity and a certain amount of disagreement. For decisions to be translated into effective actions, they must be supported by a firm commitment from people who will accept responsibility for the success of the *group* decision.

By contrast, in the non-Japanese world, there is a tendency to define the problem, to develop alternative solutions and follow this up by speedy action. The Japanese review the problem from different points of view and ask themselves "Is this really the problem?" When the problem is correctly defined, the solution emerges automatically. Periodic review via analysis of reports, communication, observations and visual inspection itself ensures success in implementation.
In the Japanese world, honesty, courtesy, kindness, and patience seem to be in abundance when compared to the rest of the world. The ability to say "I don't know" indicates a level of honesty and a willingness to learn rather than an attempt to bluff your way through business and personal life! Moreover, the latter qualities are not mistaken for signs of weakness unlike in most other parts of the globe.

**Trade Unions - Are They Evil?**

In order to run a business, one needs people, money, and time. Unlike robots, human beings have feelings and are selfish in nature. Therefore, employees should be selected on the basis of merit and duly motivated (to focus on corporate rather than personal goals), or else they will resign in terms of their attitude on the job or physically, with implications for employee turnover, costs of training, mistakes, re-establishing relationships with existing employees, and the bottom line.

Firms aim to serve all stakeholders: owners, leaders, managers, employees, customers, suppliers, the community, the government, and the general public. The resulting compromise, due to conflicts of interest, leaves a residue of profit, which firms aim to satisfice rather than maximize in the face of numerous practical considerations. Objectives include profitable growth, innovation, favorable image and goodwill, liquidity, percentage market share, reasonable safety margin, conservative financing, and effectiveness and reasonable compensation packages.

Owners and employees often believe that they have conflicting interests—they feel that the gain of one party represents a loss to the other! Both parties should state their interests in precise terms, thereby setting a foundation for successful negotiation and conflict resolution while considering *separate and common interests.* Teamwork and employee participation in decision making give employees a sense of belonging; different perspectives contribute to better decisions. However, it is difficult to alter the selfish nature of human beings and the resulting conflicts geared toward "a bigger slice of the existing pie" rather than overall welfare of the company and its associates. Hence, motivation, negotiation, and conflict resolution skills resulting in a win-win situation are of paramount importance. This will minimize labor disputes and strikes.

*A Labor Union*

A labor union consists of employees who have combined to increase bargaining power and negotiate with their employer regarding salaries and working conditions. Industrial unions include workers in a particular industry, e.g., the automobile industry. Craft unions include workers with a particular skill or craft, e.g., carpenters. Legislation aims to ensure a harmonious relationship between employers and employees, with disputes being settled in an amicable manner.

## Conciliation and Mediation

Sometimes, during a negotiation between management and unions, relations become strained, and it looks as though a strike or lockout is imminent. The government may employ full-time mediators to settle disputes and prevent strikes/lockouts. Alternatively, judges, lawyers, priests, university professors, or other professionals may be appointed as mediators or arbitrators.

Even when a contract does exist between management and unions, those who feel that they have been treated unfairly can file a "grievance," to be dealt with in accordance to the procedures established during collective bargaining. Contracts may be altered upon mutual consent.

## When All Else Fails

When it appears that a serious dispute will not be resolved,

a) *employees* may go on strike or engage in picketing—i.e., discourage customers and suppliers from dealing with the firm in question or take part in a boycott wherein members of other unions and/or the public refuse to do business with the firm; or

b) *owners or management* may enforce a lockout—i.e., prevent workers from entering the firm's premises or obtain an injunction to prevent a strike or a picket, or form an employer's association in an attempt to deal with the matters on hand.

## Some Issues in Collective Bargaining

Unions need security—certification and support of an increasing number of members—for financial and negotiating strength within a *closed shop*, wherein only union members are allowed to work in a firm/industry, or a *union shop*, wherein employees must join the union after the probationary period. Unions focus on *real* salary increases—i.e., salary increases that exceed the cost of living index (COLA), reasonable hours of work, job security, promotion, and related factors.

## Open Book Management (OBM): Sharing Information with Employees

Open book management involves sharing information with employees in the hope that brainstorming and employee participation in decision making will lead to increased profitability and benefits for all. Many organizations adopt an open book management approach in an attempt to increase corporate and individual welfare of all stakeholders.

Trust is important in any relationship and promotes win-win situations. Therefore, management and unions should build trust instead of engaging in acts that destroy trust, e.g., delay tactics or threats! Unions and management should engage in open communication and focus on mutual gains and simple solutions that consider the separate (and joint) interests of both parties.

# CHAPTER 3 – The Law, Ethics and Other Matters: *Some Pearls of Wisdom*

**The Law**

We shall refer mainly to English law, since it was in England that the law originated. The law of contract is at the heart of business law. Therefore, every businessperson must appreciate the significance of its core elements.

**The Law of Contract**

1. Offer
2. Acceptance
3. Intention to create legal relations (legal intent)
4. Consideration (except for contracts under seal)
5. Mutual consent (i.e., consent by both parties to the terms of the contract)
6. Capacity of both parties to contract
7. Legality and possibility of the contract
8. Written formalities *in some cases*

A contract is a freely negotiated agreement that is binding in law—there are *express* and *implied* terms. In the absence of one or more of the above essentials, the contract may be void, voidable, or unenforceable.

*Offer:* willingness to contract on certain terms and made to a certain person or group or to the world at large. The offer may be conditional and express or implied (e.g., public transport) and must be communicated to the offeree. Therefore, a person who returns property not knowing that a reward had been offered would not be *legally* entitled to the reward.

*Invitation to Treat:* an invitation to induce an offer, as in window displays, prospectuses, mail-order bargains, or display of goods in the supermarket.

*Lapse of Offer: upon* death of offeror or offeree before acceptance or if not accepted within the time period stipulated in the contract or "reasonable" time period as determined by the facts of each case.

*Revocation of Offer: a*n offer may be revoked if revocation is communicated to the offeree before the latter effects his or her acceptance. The same applies to an option unless the offeree has given consideration to the offeror of the option.

*Rejection of Offer: a* counter offer is a rejection of the original offer. Asking for further details is not a counter offer.

*Acceptance:* must be communicated unless the offer invites acceptance by conduct before any revocation is received from the offeror.

Acceptance must be made in the form stipulated by the offeror and, if made by post, then takes effect upon posting, even if never received by the offeror. But if handed over to a postman, it takes effect when it reaches the offeror, as in *London and Northern Bank, ex parte Jones* (1900). Acceptance may be conditional (e.g., subject to contract).


*Intention to Create Legal Relations (Legal Intent):* Legal intent must be present in order that an agreement may be regarded as a contract. In *Balfour v. Balfour* (1919), a husband agreed to pay his wife thirty dollars per month while she was abroad; this was not regarded as an intention to create legal relations *but would have been different if husband and wife had been separated.* Where more than two persons share in the stake of any open competition, there is legal intent, as in *Simpkins v. Pays* (1955). If a business agreement includes an "honorable pledge" clause (i.e., one that expressly states that the agreement is not to be legally binding), then there is no legal intent, as in *Rose and Frank v. Crompton & Bros* (1925).

*Consideration: s*omething of value rather than just "natural affection" must be given by each party to the other party. *Exception: for deeds under seal.* It may be executory, e.g., where both the parties exchange promises to perform acts in the future, or executed, e.g., where A promises to perform in return for the act of B. *An informal gratuitous promise does not amount to a contract, as confirmed by Williams v. Roffey Bros. & Nicholls (Contractors) Ltd.(1991).*

*Rules of the Doctrine of Consideration*

1. Simple contracts, *but not deeds under seal,* must be supported by consideration.
2. Consideration must have some value however small, as for chocolate wrappers in *Chappel v. Nestlé Co.* (1959).
3. Consideration must be sufficient even if inadequate—if a person attends court under subpoena and is offered a certain amount of dollars for appearing, then the individual is not *legally* entitled to payment because the latter was merely performing a legal duty by attending. If the individual performs more than a legal duty, then the latter is giving consideration, as in *Glassbrook v. Glamorgan* (1925) where mine owners asked for extra police protection from violent strikers.

An agreement by a creditor to accept less than the debt will not bind the creditor unless he receives *fresh* consideration for the discounted debt as confirmed in *Foakes v. Beer* (1884) where the creditor agreed to settlement of the debt in installments and then sued for interest and won. Fresh consideration includes another mode of payment (e.g., asset instead of cash or payment before due date or payment by third party or payment of a percentage of a disputed debt). *See also doctrine of promissory Estoppel.*

4. Consideration must be legal.

5. Consideration must be performed *after* the agreement has been made. *In Re: McArdle* (1951), an agreement to pay for repairs to a house was made after the repairs had been effected, and the consideration was regarded as *past*—therefore, there was no legal contract.
0 But where services are rendered at the request of the promisor and the latter then offers an agreeable price, the performer of the services can enforce the contract as in *Steward v. Casey* (1892).
6. Consideration must move from the promisee rather than from an outsider to the contract. See *Dunlop v. Selfridge* (1915) and *Donoghue v. Stevenson* (1932).

Consideration need not move to the promisor, as in *Re: Wyvern Developments Ltd.* (1974). Thus, the promisee may give up a job, as in *Jones v. Padavatton* (1969), or the tenancy of an apartment, as in *Coombes v. Smith* (1986), even though there is no direct benefit to the promisor.

*Promissory Estoppel*

An individual who makes a false statement that is acted upon is bound by that statement if he or she should have realized that people would have assumed the statement to be true and then acted upon the same.

*Formality:* a contract can be drafted in any form unless the

1. contract requires a deed (e.g., sale of land or interest in land), or
2. contract must be in writing or evidenced in writing (e.g., contract of guarantee).

*Contracts Requiring a Deed*

A deed is a document written on paper or on parchment or vellum (i.e., certain animal skins) and bears the seal of the person/company/entity that is bound by the deed. Where the seal belongs to a corporation, no signature is necessary in law although the corporation's regulations may stipulate that persons authorized to use the corporation's seal must sign when they use the seal. Alternatively, instead of a seal, the words *signed, sealed, and delivered* may be inserted above the signature on the document; and the latter document will then be regarded as a deed, as in *First National Securities Ltd. v. Jones* (1978).

*Capacity:* any person may enter into a contract although there are special rules regarding minors, mental patients, and registered companies.

*Minors:* a minor is defined as an individual who is less than eighteen years of age.

1. Contracts for necessaries (i.e., items that are reasonably necessary for the minor). When the necessaries are goods, the minor is only liable if the goods are

    a. suitable to the condition of his or her life,
    b. necessary to the minor at the time of sale and delivery, and
    c. goods with which the minor was not sufficiently supplied at the time of sale and delivery.
    Even if the above conditions are satisfied in the case of necessaries, the minor need pay only a *reasonable* rather than the contractual price—see *Nash v. Inman* (1908) and *Chapple v. Cooper* (1844).
2. Beneficial contracts of service. Where the contract is beneficial to the minor, the court will bind the minor (e.g., *Doyle v. White City Stadium*) unless the contract is a trading contract (e.g., *Mercantile Union v. Ball*)—a minor contractor acquired a lorry on credit terms, and this was held

not to be necessary.

3. Voidable contracts by which a minor acquires an interest of a permanent nature in, say, a share/partnership/lease binding on the minor, unless avoided during minority or within a reasonable period thereafter. The minor would have no liability for the subsequent period and may recover money paid if there has been a total failure of consideration, unlike in *Steinberg v. Scala* (1923).

4. Contracts within the Infants Relief Act 1874. The following contracts are void:
    a. For the supply of goods other than necessaries
    b. For the payment of money lent or to be lent
    c. For the repayment during majority of money lent during infancy
    d. Accounts stated (e.g., IOUs)

If a minor, X, agrees to purchase a sports car from Y for four thousand pounds and obtains usage of the car upon payment of a deposit of four hundred pounds and then sells the car to Z, then Y cannot obtain the balance of £3,600 from X or the car from Z *unless the goods are necessaries or beneficial items.*

*Terms*

A representation is a statement of fact that is made before a contract is executed in order to persuade a person to enter into contract. A term is an integral part of the contract itself.

*Conditions and Warranties*

Breach of condition is tantamount to breach of contract because a condition is fundamental to a contract, as defined in *Wallis v. Pratt* (1911), whereas a warranty is not fundamental to the contract. Breach of condition entitles the injured party to repudiate the contract whereas breach of warranty entitles the injured party to damages only.

*Express and Implied Terms*

In general, a written agreement carries more weight than an oral agreement regarding the same matter; but this rule of parole evidence, which relates to express terms, is subject to exceptions, as in *Humphrey v. Dale* (1857). Implied terms may originate from

1. custom unless expressly ruled out by the nature of the contract, as in *Hutton v. Warren* (1836);
2. statute as in the sale of goods being governed by the Sale of Goods Acts 1979;
3. judicial interpretation of the contract, as in *Lister v. Romford Ice and Cold Storage* (1957) and the *Moorcock* (1889).

*Exclusion Clauses*

Where such exclusion of liability clauses are included in standard printed forms used by businessmen, it is essential to establish whether the exclusion clause

1. is a term of the contract, having been accepted by signature of the client.
2. covers loss that has occurred to the defendant, who deserves to be compensated.
3. is inoperative on certain grounds, e.g., where it is misleading or unfair.

We shall consider ways in which a contract may be *discharged*.

## Mistake

Relief from a transaction may follow from a mistake of *fact* rather than of *law*. There are three possible types of mistake:

1. Common mistake. Where each party makes the same mistake, thus canceling the contract, as in *Strickland v. Turner* (1852) where A bought an annuity from B on a person C, who (unknown to either A or B) was already dead; and as in *Cooper v. Phibbs* (1867) where A contracted to buy from B a lease on a property, which, unknown to either party, already belonged to A. Equity may allow a person to avoid such a contract on fair grounds proposed by the court. *Where an oral contract is substantiated by a contradictory written contract, equity may allow rectification of the latter on the grounds of fairness.*

2. Mutual mistake. Where each party makes a different mistake, they are at cross-purposes, as in *Raffles v. Wickelhaus* (1864) where there was no agreement re the subject matter of the contract; two ships named *Peerless* arrived from Bombay and in *Wood v. Scarth* (1855) where A intended to earn a premium on rented property but did not inform B, who accepted the offer of a lease at $x per annum.

3. Unilateral mistake. Where one party is mistaken and the other party knows or is presumed to know of the mistake—where fraud is involved, the contract may be declared void; or the plaintiff may be able to sue for misrepresentation, depending upon the circumstances. In *Cundy v. Lindsay* (1878), A (a crook) posed and signed as a representative of Messrs. Blenkiron & Co., received goods from X, and sold them to Y, who bought them in good faith. X sued, and it was held that Y had no right to X's goods.

In *Lewis v. Averay* (1972), the crook who posed as an actor and signed a check was able to pass on title. The contract was declared voidable for fraud rather than void for unilateral mistake. The goods could not be recovered from the innocent third party, as in the case of *Philip v. Brooks* (1919).

## *Non est Factum*

*Non est factum* is an attempt to deny the contract on the grounds that "it is not my deed"—the court will consider the following points:

1. The pleader must not have been negligent when entering into the contract although infirmity, illiteracy, blindness, or senility may be accepted in mitigation.

2. The signed document and the end result should be contrary to the pleader's intentions when the contract was entered into.

## Misrepresentation

A representation is a statement of fact or past event made with a view to encouraging a contract. A representation of intention is not actionable unless it implies fact whereas a representation of law cannot found an action merely because it happens to be wrong unless it implies a basis of fact as in *West London Commercial Bank v. Kitson* (1884).

In *Edgington v. Fitzmaurice* (1885), A lent company B some money to improve the latter company's buildings and facilitate expansion. The directors, instead, used the money to pay off the company's creditors and were held liable in deceit. *A statement of opinion is not a representation normally.*

A representation must normally be via positive words or conduct rather than by silence or nondisclosure but pay special attention to the following situations:

1. Where there is a half-truth, as in *Tapp v. Lee* (1803)
2. Where true statements become false before conclusion of the contract, as in *With v. O'Flanagan* (1936)
3. Where there is a fiduciary or confidential relationship between parties, as in *Tate v. Williamson* (1866)
4. Where the contract is one of *uberrimae fidei*, or utmost good faith.

### *Contracts Uberrimae Fidei (Utmost Good Faith)*

In contracts of *uberrimae fidie*, the parties must disclose *all material facts*; otherwise, the contract may be rescinded, as in the classic case of insurance where the insured must disclose the relevant facts. *Uberrimae fidei* also applies to contracts between members of a family where the contract benefits the family, as in *Greenwood v. Greenwood* (1863).

### *Types of Misrepresentation*
Misrepresentation may be as follows:

1. Fraudulent if made to mislead or not believing it to be true or reckless—remedy: rescission or refusal to perform, *plus* damages
2. Innocent if the party making the statement honestly believed the same to be true:
.1a. negligently—remedy as in 1 above
.2b. non-negligently—remedy as in 1 above; damages may be granted in lieu of rescission.

### *Rescission*

A contract may not be rescinded where

1. the injured party has affirmed the contract or benefited from it;
2. there had been an undue lapse of time, which implied affirmation, as in *Leaf v. International Galleries* (1950);

3. the parties cannot be restored to their original positions; and
4. third-party rights have accrued.

## *Duress and Undue Influence*

Duress is an attempt to force a person to act against his or her own free will and may be economic in nature. The party threatened or unduly influenced may treat the contract as voidable, subject to certain rules.

## *Contracts in Restraint of Trade*

A contract in restraint of trade, profession, or calling is prima facie void unless it is reasonably in the interests of the parties or the public at large.

*Severance*

If some clauses are severable, the courts may apply the "blue pencil" test (i.e., may uphold some of the clauses). In *Nordenfelt v. Maxim Nordenfelt Guns and Ammunition Co. Ltd.* (1894), A, an inventor and manufacturer of guns and ammunition, sold his or her business to B and contracted not to compete with B for twenty-five years

1. by making guns or ammunition anywhere in the world or
2. in any other way.
   *The court supported 1 only.*

## Discharge of Contract

A contract may be discharged/terminated by

1. joint agreement,
2. performance,
3. breach,
4. frustration (i.e., subsequent impossibility),
5. lapse of time, or
6. operation of law.

## Remedies for Breach of Contract

1. Damages. Ordinary damages may be awarded for actual loss suffered so long as the loss is not too remote, as in *Hadley v. Baxendale* (1854) where A was not aware that by delaying the repair of B's tools, B would suffer a loss of profits.

   In *Victoria Laundry v. Newman* (1949), A bought a boiler from B for A's laundry, but B delayed delivery by five months. So A sued for

   a. loss of profits during the delay and

b. loss of two highly profitable contracts during the delay.

The latter was considered too remote, but A succeeded in item a.

In *Diamond v. Campbell Jones* (1961), A contracted to sell property to B but then changed his mind. B sued for profit lost as a result and A had to pay the market value less sale price agreed upon with B.

The plaintiff must always try to minimize his or her post-tax damages, as confirmed by *Brace v. Calder* (1895) where A had been employed as a manager of a firm B, which consisted of four partners, two of whom subsequently died. The surviving partners, wishing to continue, offered A a technical dismissal linked to an offer of reemployment. A sued for wrongful dismissal and received only nominal damages because A had not attempted to mitigate his or her loss.

If the contract provides that, upon breach, a certain amount of sterling pounds will be payable as damages (i.e., *liquidated* damages), then the court will enforce the sum if it is a reasonable measure of the *actual* loss suffered rather than an excess amount (i.e., a *penalty*).

2. Specific performance. This equitable remedy may be granted at the court's discretion unless

   a. damages are adequate,
   b. the court cannot adequately supervise performance as in contracts of employment,
   c. there is no consideration,
   d. one of the parties is a minor,
   e. the contract is for a loan of money,
   f. the plaintiff did not perform in accordance with his or her obligations.
3. Injunction. This equitable remedy restrains a person from performing a tortuous act or an act, which is in contravention to the contract.

4. Rescission. This equitable remedy restores the plaintiff and the defendant to their positions before the contract unless A receives money from B as a guarantee for B's performance; and B then commits breach of contract, in which case, A will probably be allowed to retain the guarantee money.
5. Refusal of further performance. The injured party can use the breach as his or her defense against refusal to perform further and may ask for rescission.
6. *Quantum Meruit*. In addition to what was discussed earlier, a *quantum meruit* claim may also succeed in a contract that is subsequently found to be void, as in *Craven-Ellis* v. Canons Limited (1936) where there was a quasi contract.

7. Promissory estoppel has already been discussed.

**Other Matters Relating to Contracts**

We rarely think about life beyond the contract, but there are potential problems related to

1. the handover,
2. the transition,
3. continuity,
4. change management, and
5. termination and exit.

Performance must be monitored to ensure that it does not deviate from what was agreed upon and to ensure that contractors do not take shortcuts or resources out of the project to increase their profit margins or to service other customers. Normally, end-user organizations have a changing rather than a fixed set of requirements, and there are issues that must be dealt with in order to mitigate postcontract risks. Organizations must keep referring to the contract and amend it to reflect changes required as the project progresses. Constant communication will help maintain the integrity of the contract while obtaining value for money and adding to the bottom line.

Record everything including conversations and discussions at meetings. Evidence may take the form of hard copies, electronic documents, handwritten notes, videos, and software. A businessman must have the ability to sense trouble (if he cannot avoid trouble), and he must attempt to settle disputes out of court where practical. One is advised to minimize conflicts and hasten the conflict resolution process.

**The Nature of Contract**

The rules governing the formation of contracts are complex. Where a dispute arises between the parties to a contract, litigation or arbitration may be necessary to determine the rights of the parties. *The law states that any way you would want to record your contract is fine as long as both parties have prior agreement on the format, except for the sale of land.*

The Electronic Communications and Transactions (ECT) Act 2002 (South Africa) paved the way for businesses to move away from paper-based contracts to electronic format (e.g., e-mail or a Word document), which will enable a central online repository for tracking contracts. The ECT Act states that if a contracting party wants to retain a copy of the contract in an electronic form, then party must meet the following requirements:

1. The information must be accessible and used subsequent to the signing of the contract.
2. The contract must be in the format in which it was generated or in a format that can be demonstrated to accurately represent the contract.
3. The origin and destination of the contract as well as the date and time it was sent or received must be determinable.

**Signatures on the Contract**

In order for an electronic agreement to be considered the original, the contract must be unaltered and capable of being displayed or produced.

**Signed and Sealed**

A contract is a legal agreement that must be signed for validation. With regard to electronic signatures, the ECT Act requires that advanced electronic signatures are preferable, depending on the legal agreement between the parties. Two major technologies that ensure legally acceptable electronic signatures are public key infrastructure digital signatures and click-wrap agreements.

**Hard Copies and Electronic Copies**

Businesses should store their documents in accordance with the statute of limitations, i.e., normally up to six years unless fraud is involved. It is advisable to convert old hard copies to electronic formats as backup. If all new contracts are electronically originated with electronic signatures or click-wrap agreements, then perhaps the paperless contract has come of age.

Concurrent delay arises where a project has been delayed because of two or more events that operate at the same time—one of the events is the responsibility of the project owner, and the other is the responsibility of the contractor. For example, an owner instructs a contractor to undertake additional work via a change order, with the understanding that this will delay completion of the project in question. However, at the time of carrying out the additional work, the contractor has reduced its labor resources for reasons unrelated to the variation. The additional work and insufficient resources run concurrently delay completion of the project.

The question arises as to who is responsible for the one-month delay in completion of the project. Is it the contractor, in which case, the owner will be entitled to claim its delay-related damages? Or is it the responsibility of the owner, in which case, the contractor will be relieved from liquidated damages by extending the time for completion and may also recover its delay-related losses—prolongation, disruption, and acceleration costs? Or is responsibility to be shared between the parties, and on what basis?

An insight was found in the English decision of *Henry Boot Construction (UK) Ltd. v. Malmaison Hotel (Manchester) Ltd.* (1999). The judgment noted the common ground between the parties that if there are two concurrent causes of delay, one of which is a relevant event (e.g., the owner's change order) and the other is not (e.g., the contractor's insufficient resources), the contractor is entitled to an extension of time for the delay caused by the relevant event. *The Malmaison Hotel case does not provide guidance on how the extension of time should be quantified in a situation involving concurrent delays.* (Also see *Royal Brompton Hospital NHS Trust v. Hammond and Others* [2001] where the contractor was "entitled to extensions of time by reason of . . . relevant events, notwithstanding its own defaults.")

Possible bases of measurement advanced at an academic level include the following (see

John Marrin, QC, "Concurrent Delay," paper given to the Society of Construction Law Hong Kong (March 18, 2003):

1. Apportionment. Allocation of the time and money effects of the delay to project completion based on the relative significance of the competing causes of delay
2. The American approach. The contractor is granted an extension of time but does not recover delay-related loss and damage related to his own actions/omissions (i.e., a "zero sum" outcome)
3. "But for" test. A simplistic argument arising from the principles of causation in tort cases, which ignores the contractor's delays and asserts that "but for" the owner-caused delay, the contract completion would not have overrun
4. The dominant-cause approach. Using principles of causation and contract law to emphasize the dominant cause of the delay in completion of the project (i.e., only one delay event is determined to be the cause of the delay)

*The City Inn Appeal*

The Scottish appeal decision of *City Inn Limited v. Shepherd Construction Limited* (2007) lays down that concurrent delays should be dealt with by apportioning responsibility based on what is fair and reasonable as outlined below.

**E-mail Contracts**

Parties can conclude a contract or amend an existing contract via e-mail. In *Hostcentric Technologies Inc. v. Republic Thunderbolt, LLC*, USA (2005), in a dispute over a commercial lease, the plaintiff tenant sought to enforce a settlement agreement documented in an e-mail exchange against the landlord defendant.

On September 21, 2004, after litigation had begun, the landlord's attorney sent an e-mail to the tenant's lawyer "to confirm my client's final settlement counter-proposal: . . . a $755,000 payment by the tenant, with the landlord retaining the security deposit, and for the tenant to remove its property from the premises within 21 days at its own expense." The pending action "would be dismissed with prejudice and all parties would exchange mutual general releases. The payment is due my client within 10 days from today's date." The e-mail added that the counterproposal "expires by 9:30 a.m. tomorrow, unless accepted by you before that time," and it ended with the attorney's first name.

Later that evening, the tenant's attorney sent an e-mail to the landlord's attorney to accept the offer, stating, "I am writing to formally accept your settlement offer as set forth by you in your message from earlier this evening below." The e-mail added, "[t]his matter is now conclusively settled. Please let me know how you would like to communicate this fact to the Court." The action was subsequently dismissed, but the settlement contained an indemnification clause that the tenant refused to accept.

The tenant maintained that the e-mailed offer and acceptance formed a valid settlement agreement, but the landlord disagreed "in the absence of a fully executed, written agreement . . . the e-mails concerned the monetary accord and did not finally resolve the scope of the release and other issues."

Held: The September 21, 2004, e-mails were enforceable under contract law. The landlord sent the tenant a "final settlement counterproposal" with an expiration date to accept the offer and listed all the essential terms of the settlement: the amount, removal of property from the premises, mutual general releases, and dismissal of the lawsuit. The tenant accepted the offer within that time frame, e-mailing the landlord to "formally accept your settlement offer" and stating that the matter was "now conclusively settled." Neither of the parties expressed (or implied) his or her intention not to be bound by the e-mail exchange!

*Signature Requirement*

*JSO Assoc. Inc. v. Price*, USA (2008), confirms that e-mail contracts can comply with the New York Statute of Frauds, General Obligations Law. The court agreed that e-mail correspondence constituted a sufficient memorandum of the contract since it "identifies the parties to the contract, the subject matter . . . and establishes that the plaintiff in fact performed."

The court noted that the terms of the agreement may be established by a combination of signed and unsigned documents or other writings that bear the signature of the party to be charged or his agent, and the unsigned document refers to the same transaction. Here, one of the defendants sent an e-mail to one of the plaintiffs about a proposed transaction. In the e-mail, the defendant stated, "I'm impressed . . . Let's talk this morning . . . tell me what you want for bringing this together."

The following morning, the plaintiff sent an e-mail to the defendant entitled "A Few Questions" and added that he had urged two other individuals to "come up with a cash advance . . . to make the deal." The court had to decide whether there was a "signed" agreement. Held: The defendant's name appeared in the e-mail address at the top of the message, but the e-mail closed, "I'll talk to you later"; and except for the defendant's name in the e-mail address, it was otherwise *unsigned*.

The court noted a forty-year-old decision by the Appellate Division, Second Department: "The subscription which the statute [of frauds] demands is a writing at the end of the memorandum . . . rather than a scrawl at the top of the memorandum." But the Supreme Court declared that that case was decided in a different technological era when e-mail and home computers had not even entered the public imagination. Also, the requirement of a signature at the bottom was to minimize the possibility of fraudulent additions to the memorandum, a practice that is not feasible with electronic communication.

The court noted that "electronic signatures" on formal documents such as tax returns or SEC filings are now common. Accordingly, where there was no question as to the source and authenticity of an e-mail, which was "signed" for purposes of the statute of frauds if the defendant's name "appears in the e-mail as the sender." Because the defendant's name appeared as the sender of the e-mail (and because the defendant had sent another e-mail concerning the deal that he ended with his first name "in the traditional letter writing fashion"), the statute of frauds' signature requirement was satisfied.

## Contract Modification

*Stevens v. Publicis, S.A.* (2008) confirmed that e-mail communications could serve to modify an existing contract. The plaintiff sold his New York-based public relations firm to the defendant, a French global communications company, and its codefendant U.S. subsidiary. The sale involved two contracts: a stock purchase agreement, which transferred all the plaintiff company's stock to the defendants, and an employment agreement, which allowed the plaintiff to continue as chairman and chief executive officer of the new company for three years. The plaintiff's duties were to be the "customary duties of a Chief Executive Officer."

After the acquisition, financial problems appeared. The plaintiff and a representative of the defendants exchanged e-mails, culminating in a message from the defendants' representative, stating his understanding of the terms regarding plaintiff's new role in the company. The plaintiff "accepted the proposal" and the defendants' representative affirmed the defendants' commitment to the modified arrangement. Each of the e-mail transmissions bore the name of the sender at the foot of the message.

The court held that the parties had agreed in writing to modify plaintiff's duties under the employment agreement, based upon the e-mail exchange between the parties in which both sides accepted the modification to the agreement. The e-mails from the plaintiff constituted "signed writings" within the meaning of the statute of frauds since the plaintiff's name at the end of his e-mail "signified his intent to authenticate the contents." Similarly, the defendants' representative's name at the end of his e-mail constituted a "signed writing" and meant that the employment contract of the plaintiff had been duly modified.

*Parties wishing to avoid the impact of a ruling that e-mail communications have created contractual obligations (or have amended an existing contract) should make their intentions clear in their e-mail messages.*

## Choice of Law and Choice of Jurisdiction

Many contracts contain a "choice of *law*" clause, which specifies the law that will be used to interpret the contract. Such clauses are subject to judicial interference! The Rome Convention (which has been incorporated into English law via the Contracts [Applicable Law] Act 1990). Article 5(2) of the convention provides that the choice of law made by the parties shall not . . . deprive the consumer of the protection afforded to him by the mandatory rules of the law of the country in which he habitually resides:

— if in that country the conclusion of the contract was preceded by a specific invitation

addressed to him or by advertising, and he had taken in that country all the steps necessary on his part for the conclusion of the contract, or
— if the other party or his agent received the consumer's order in that country, or
— if the contract is for the sale of goods and the consumer travelled from that country to another country and there gave his order, provided that the consumer's journey was arranged by the seller for the purpose of inducing the consumer to buy.

Where the courts are unable to identify an express or implied choice of law, the governing law will be that law that is most closely connected to the contract. Article 4(2) of the Rome Convention provides the following:

> *It shall be presumed that the contract is most closely connected with the country where the party who is to effect the performance ... at the time of conclusion of the contract, his habitual residence, or, in the case of a body corporate or unincorporated, its central administration is located. However, if the contract is entered into in the course of that party's trade or profession, that country shall be the country in which the principal place of business is situated or, where under the terms of the contract the performance is to be effected through a place of business other than the principal place of business, the country in which that other place of business is situated. There are some exceptions to this general rule.*

*When parties negotiate the terms of an international sale, they usually include a choice of law clause in their contract; but the parties may realize later on that the law, which ultimately applies to their contract, is not the law that they meant to apply. Why is that?*

## Contracts for the International Sale of Goods 1980 (CISG)

In 1980, the United Nations Commission on International Trade Law introduced the United Nations Convention on Contracts for the International Sale of Goods 1980 (CISG), ak.a. the Vienna Sales Convention, to enable fairness in international trade through a system of uniform sale of goods rules.

*When does the CISG apply?*
The CISG applies to sale of goods (*not services*) between parties from different states if
1. the parties have specifically chosen the CISG to govern their contract,
2. the parties have chosen the law of one of the contracting states to govern their contract,
3. both parties are residents in contracting states (if parties have made no explicit choice), or
4. the relevant conflict of laws rules lead to the application of the law of a contracting state.

The second situation is the most likely. The CISG applies if the parties have agreed that the contract be governed by the law of a contracting state. To date, the CISG has more than seventy signatories (or contracting states), including Australia, China, Germany, Korea, the Russian Federation, New Zealand, and the United States of America. Accordingly, if the substantive law clause in a contract points to one of the laws of those countries the CISG applies. If the parties have not specifically agreed upon a law to apply to their contract, CISG will probably apply. The following scenarios show situations in which the CISG is applicable:

*Scenario 1:* Japanese car parts manufacturer and Australian importer enter into a sales and delivery contract choosing Singaporean law to apply to their contract.

*Scenario 2:* An Australian resources company and a Chinese steel manufacturer enter into a contract for the delivery of iron ore to China, specifying the laws in Western Australia to govern their contract.

*Scenario 3:* Australian seller and Indonesian purchaser enter into a sales contract without choosing a specific law to govern their contract.

In scenario 1, the CISG applies because the parties have agreed to the application of the laws of Singapore, a contracting state even if Japan is not a signatory to the CISG.

In scenario 2, the CISG applies as the parties have agreed that the laws in Western Australia shall govern their contract. Each of the states and territories in Australia has incorporated the CISG into their legislation.

In scenario 3, the CISG applies because of private international law (conflict of laws), which (in most situations) will point to the law of the seller—in this case, Australia, a contracting state—as the law that has the closest connection to the transaction.

The CISG does not apply to

1. goods bought for private use;
2. goods sold by auction;
3. the sale of shares;
4. stocks and investment securities;
5. the sale of ships, vessels, or aircrafts; and
6. contracts for the sale of electricity.

Sales at commodity exchanges are not in the above-mentioned categories. Therefore, the CISG applies.

The CISG is also excluded for contracts where the main obligation of the supplier consists of the supply of labor and services (e.g., turnkey contracts). As far as construction or infrastructure contracts are concerned, one must analyze the predominant obligations (service and labor /delivery of goods) to determine whether the CISG applies.

*How to Exclude the CISG*

The CISG applies unless the parties choose to exclude it explicitly (e.g., by stating "The laws of [state], excluding the CISG, shall apply"). Before excluding the CISG, consider the following matters. During the last three decades, the CISG has increased in prominence in both arbitral and court proceedings. The CISG governs contract formation, the obligation of the contracting parties, the formalities regarding contracts, and remedies available for the breach of contract. Parties can negotiate their rights and obligations under the contract and tailor their risk and reward scenarios to a particular transaction.

*Electronic Communications and Related Laws*

The law relating to electronic communications continues to evolve. In *JSO Associates Inc. v. Price*, USA (2008), Justice Stephen A. Bucaria held that e-mail messages exchanged between the parties satisfied the statute of frauds. Justice Bucaria found that the Mexican corporate defendant was "transacting business" within New York, based on the Court of Appeals' decisions in *Fischbarg v. Douce* (2007) and *Deutsche Bank Securities Inc. v. Montana Bd. of Investments* (2006). In both cases, the Court of Appeals relied on electronic communications to support New York's jurisdiction over out-of-state defendants.

## The Statute of Frauds

To satisfy the statute of frauds, "the terms of the agreement may be established by a combination of signed and unsigned documents, letters, or other writings provided that the writing establishing a contractual relationship between the parties bears the signature of the party to be charged or his agent and the unsigned document refers on its face to the same transaction as that set forth in the one that was signed," citing *Intercontinental Planning, Ltd. v. Daystrom Inc.*, USA (1969).

After reviewing cases before the "electronic age," Justice Bucaria adopted a practical, commonsense approach to the question of e-mails being sufficient to satisfy the statute of frauds. Based on the rather mechanical manner in which other courts have analyzed similar issues, Justice Bucaria's practical approach was not without question.

In *Parma Tile Mosaic & Marble Co. Inc. v. Estate of Short*, USA (1996), the court held that a fax transmission guaranteeing payment did not satisfy the statute of frauds' requirement that the writing be "subscribed" because the defendant did not "sign" the fax. Automatic imprinting of the sender's name at the top of the fax transmittal did not constitute "a signature" or "an intent, actual or apparent, to authenticate [the] writing."

In *Rosenfeld v. Zerneck*, USA (2004) it was determined that e-mails can be sufficient to satisfy statute of frauds requirements relating to transactions concerning real property.

## Analysis of the Substance of the Contract

In *JSO Associates*, Justice Bucaria analyzed the substance of the relevant e-mails rather than the technical issues: whether the e-mail contained the defendant's "signature" at the bottom. He held "that where there is no question as to the source and authenticity of an email—the email is 'signed' for purposes of the statute of frauds if defendant's name clearly appears in the email as the sender." Justice Bucaria noted that "the requirement of a signature at the bottom was to minimize the opportunity for fraudulent additions to the memorandum, a practice which is not feasible with electronic communication." He referred to the U.S. Court of

Appeals decision in *Cloud Corp. v. Hasbro Inc.*, USA (2002): "the sender's name on an e-mail satisfies the signature requirement of the statute of frauds."

With these principles in mind, Justice Bucaria found that the e-mails sent by the defendant to the plaintiff sufficiently supported the existence of a contract, identified the subject matter of the alleged brokerage agreement, and tied in all defendants to the alleged contract. The court also found that in some e-mail messages, the defendant's name appeared as the sender while in other relevant e-mail, the defendant had typed his name at the end "in the traditional letter writing fashion."

**Agency**

An agent is a person who has the authority plus capacity to create legal relations between his or her principal and any third party; his or her actions bind the principal so long as the actions are agreed upon in a contract between agent and principal. A minor agent will bind an adult principal, but not vice versa—see *G(A) v. G(T)* (1970).

*Creation of Agency*

1. By express agreement. The agent may be appointed orally/in writing/by deed. Only when appointed by deed can the agent execute a deed. The agent is called the attorney, and the deed that appointed him or her is called the power of attorney.

2. By implication. Where an individual is placed in a situation that would normally appear to confer on him or her, the capacity of an agent (e.g., a person appointed to act as a land agent) may have implied authority to sign tenancy agreements on behalf of his or her employer.

In *Watteau v. Fenwick* (1893), A sold a public house to B but continued as manager and bought cigars on credit from C although forbidden to do so (by B). C was unable to claim payment from A, who C believed to be the owner of the public house, but could claim the price from B, the present owner, because cigars would normally be supplied to a public house. Agency by implication also arises where A buys from B who is normally paid by C for A's purchase—therefore, C will be stopped from denying that A is his/ her agent unless C expressly informs B accordingly.

3. By necessity. The individual who deals with /possesses another individual's property may be allowed to protect the owner's interest without specific instructions from the latter person for the following:

a. It was impossible to obtain the owner's instructions, as in *Great Northern Railway v. Swaffield* (1874) where A carried a horse to its destination, and nobody arrived to collect the same. So A put the horse in a nearby stable and charged the owner, B, for the same. The court allowed the charges to B because A acted in B's interest in an emergency.

b. There was a valid reason.

c. The agent acted bona fide on behalf of the owner.

4. By ratification. A principal may ratify a contract made with a third party by a person hitherto unauthorized to act as the former's agent for the following:

    a. The "agent" informs the third party that he/she is acting for the specific first party, unlike the situation in *Keighley, Maxsted and Co. v. Durrant* (1901) and *Watson v. Swann* (1862).

    b. The principal was capable of contracting at the time of the contract. In *Kelner v. Baxter* (1866), the company was not formed at the time of the contract. Therefore, the individuals who purported to have acted on the company's behalf were personally liable for the contract they signed, and the situation was similar in *Phonogram v. Lane* (1982).

    c. The principal ratifies the whole and valid contract within the time fixed for ratification or within a reasonable time and is aware of all material facts as confirmed by *Savery v. King* (1856). The ratified contract is effective from the date of contract made by the agent. In *Bolton Partner v. Lambert* (1889), A could not revoke an offer (which was accepted by B's agent) before ratification by B.

    5. By estoppel. If A allows B to give an impression that B represents A, then A will be bound by B's actions (i.e., A will be estopped from denying that B is A's agent).

Where A ceases to be a partner of a firm, A should inform all concerned parties; otherwise, some of them might deal with the firm in the belief that A is still a partner, and A could be held responsible for the firm's commitments in such cases.

## Relationship between Agent and Principal

    1. Duties of an agent:

    a. Obedience to his or her principal's lawful instructions, as confirmed by *Turpin v. Bilton* (1843) and *Cohen v. Kittel* (1889)

    b. Due skill and care, as confirmed by *Keppel v. Wheeler* (1927)

    c. Utmost good faith whereby the agent is not allowed to compete with his or her principal or gain a benefit from the contract unknown to the principal, as confirmed by *Grimsted v. Hadrill* (1953) and *Reading v. Attorney General* (1951), or misuse confidential info gained regarding his or her principal's affairs

    d. Duties to be carried out personally rather than through another party unless so authorized expressly or by implication by his or her principal, as confirmed by *De Bussche v. Art* (1878); or where the act is purely ministerial and does not involve confidence or discretion, as in *Allan v. Europa* (1968); or where allowed by custom/ trade; or where there were unforeseen circumstances faced by the agent

    e. Accounts to be rendered to the principal

    2. Duties of the principal:

    a. Commission to agent

.1b. Expenses of agent to be reimbursed

    3. Rights of agent against principal:

    a. Lien on goods according to the type of agency (e.g., factor, auctioneer)

    b. Stoppage of goods in transit to the principal if agent is responsible for payment, and there is a net amount owed by principal to agent

*Termination of Agency*

    1. Act of the parties:

a. Mutual agreement and discharge
   b. Unilaterally (unless irrevocable) and upon due notice in line with the agency contract; otherwise, the injured party may action the contract
2. Operation of law upon illness, death, bankruptcy of either party, or destruction of the subject matter of the contract
3. Completion of the agency agreement

*Effect of Revocation*

If an agent continues to act as agent after revocation of his or her authority, then a third party may sue him or her for breach of warranty of authority. If an agent's authority is by deed (i.e., power of attorney), then the agent and persons dealing with him or her are protected if the agent's authority is revoked without their knowledge (e.g., by death [unknown to them] of the principal). (See the Enduring Powers of Attorney Act 1985.)

*Irrevocable Agency*

If authorization of agent is by deed or for valuable consideration, it can be revoked only upon the obligation being discharged but not by illness, death, or bankruptcy of principal. Therefore, if A borrows from B and authorizes the latter to sell A's property and repay the loan, then A cannot revoke his or her authorization to B until the loan is repaid.

## Ethics

Ethics goes beyond the law, in the sense that conscience should dictate one's actions in an attempt to "do the right thing" even if the law does not require you to. For instance, if an employee has freely, i.e., without duress, agreed to work for a company for $52,000.00 per year and if it is obvious that the employee in question deserves much more, then additional amounts should be forthcoming in relation to what is truly believed to be fair.

## Anger Management

Anger is a normal emotion which must be controlled, otherwise this emotion can cause problems for oneself and others within one's circle. You could be angry at a co-worker or because of a situation such as a traffic jam or a canceled flight or upon recalling traumatic or enraging events. A certain amount of anger is necessary for survival. Anger can be handled by expressing one's feelings, suppressing one's feelings or calming down. Deep breathing, relaxing imagery, yoga and other forms of meditation can help in calming down a person, as can additional leisure time, entertainment, sightseeing and holidays.

*Improved Communication*

Listen carefully and ascertain the cause(s) of anger e.g., you like more freedom and personal space, but your partner wants more closeness. If he or she starts complaining, respond to her needs instead of criticizing her.

*Humour, Changing Your Environment, Lifestyle, Diet and the Need for Adequate Sleep*

Humor can defuse rage but should not be offensive. Try to picture what you are saying so that you can benefit from the visual impact of your verbal expressions. Immediate surroundings, problems, lifestyle, a low level of intimacy, responsibilities, the quest for perfection and your sleep pattern and current diet can contribute to your anger and must be monitored in order to be more effective in life.

**Ethics, Legal Implications and Reputation**

Uncontrolled demonstrations of anger can have ethical and legal implications, as can be seen from the examples of Naomi Campbell and Russell Crowe. At one of his rock concert performances, Crowe threw in a humorous twist, by displaying a golden replica of the telephone he had thrown at a hotel employee a few years ago. Also, while hosting the Australian Film Industry Awards, Crowe showed the audience an old-fashioned telephone and added that "If there are any problems and you do get up here and go on too long, then (say) 'hello' to my little friend." Crowe believes that anger is a prerequisite for survival and that "…holding and suppressing (anger) is…bull----."

**Conclusion**

The world seems to abound with business organizations that focus on immediate gains regardless of ethical and legal considerations and individuals who create problems because of their inability to control their temper. Corporate performance is being undermined by workplace bullying and related stress in the work place. These issues must be addressed in a timely manner otherwise there will be dire consequences which can be avoided.

# CHAPTER 4 – Some Final Thoughts on Leadership

**Humor**

Research in the field of management has led us to believe that stress is one of the main factors influencing performance on a personal and corporate level. Stress exists because of problems encountered by people at home, at work and elsewhere. Therefore, in order to improve performance, managers must realize that they have to reduce, or (possibly) eliminate, stress from the work environment. A good sense of humour definitely helps in this context.

**Change and the Ability to Manage Change**

Change should rest on a solid foundation of reason, and the people, who will be affected by the change, should be informed of its significance in advance of implementation, thus minimizing or eliminating emotional andr other disturbances. Leaders should ensure that employees and trade unions understand and appreciate the need for the required change and cooperate accordingly. Hopefully, change will lead to an increase in overall welfare.

**Telecommuting**

In an attempt to cut costs while enabling individuals to enjoy the convenience of working from home, many organizations are offering sub-contracting opportunities which appear to be quite attractive but involve a minimum financial investment by the organizations in question. Individuals with the required capabilities are often tempted to take advantage of such opportunities, which eliminate the need for commuting to and from work and the stress related thereto, especially in conditions of inclement weather, the need to dress up, take food from home or buy food at a restaurant on a daily basis, etc. The latter are often pointed out as being some of the benefits of working from home.

**Workplace Bullying**

Targets, victims and witnesses of bullying face increased levels of stress when subjected to obvious *repeated* acts of rudeness or aggression, malicious rumours, exclusion socially or from certain projects, undue criticism of work, opinions, habits, attitudes, or private life and intrusion upon privacy. In North America, although bullying is recognized as detrimental to occupational health, there is little political or corporate interest in stopping it.
Reporting a bully to the HR department may expose the target, victim or witness of bullying to the risk of even more bullying, slower career advancement, or even termination, on the grounds of being a "troublemaker!" Workplace bullying has severe consequences, including reduced effectiveness and high employee turnover. An employee who suffers any physical or psychiatric injury as a result of workplace bullying can confront the bully, report the bully to the HR department or to the trade union, if any, sue the employer and the abusive employee as joint respondents in the claim. Training sessions can raise awareness and ethical IQs, but it is difficult to alter the basic nature of some individuals, who may need counselling.

**Undergraduates Seeking Work Experience**

Undergraduates often believe that they can increase their marketability by gaining suitable work experience prior to graduation. Employers, being aware of this, often try to gain an unfair advantage by offering them *unpaid* jobs during their vacations. In my opinion, these graduates should be offered at least the legally permissible minimum wage.

**Teamwork**

Teamwork can be defined as the collective action of a group of individuals in pursuit of a common goal (or set of goals). Individuals are selfish in nature in terms of focusing on their own personal goals. Therefore, leaders must care for them and motivate them to perform in accordance with corporate objectives and related plans. Members of a team should be allowed to participate in brainstorming, decision making and profits, in an ethical manner.
*People are the life-giving element in any organization.* The success of a business enterprise is definitely a function of its employees, who constitute the main investment (rather than an army of slaves), even in the presence of competent owners and managers. A business enterprise needs dynamic team players with excellent communication and interpersonal skills, different professional and cultural backgrounds, and perspectives emanating therefrom. Owners,

managers, employees and other stakeholders should be receptive to the views of others in an attempt to make the right decisions, rather than merely inflate their personal egos! Making the right move is far more important than simply satisfying one's ego, the cost of which could be astronomical. Members of a team may change, according to the goal in mind, but they should complement, rather than compete with, one another while focusing on the objective at hand!

Andrew Carnegie was a great team builder, because he selected better people than himself and always encouraged peak performance through synergy and a positive attitude. Instead of hiring employees who are less capable than yourself, in an attempt to safeguard your position and your family income, hire the best. Then lead these employees by example, motivate them with meaningful work, increase their responsibility, give them challenges and rewards, and empathize with them when necessary. Do not merely give them a smile, verbal praise, a pat on the back and a cheap lunch when teamwork results in added profits for the business organization! Motivated employees will contribute to profitable growth and overall welfare. Members of a business enterprise should have the ability to interact favorably with people of different nationalities and cultures while always respecting their values.

*The customer should always be considered as part of the team because he or she is a stakeholder.* Encourage feedback from customers, research into their needs and wants, and do your best to satisfy them, *while bearing in mind that they are not always right.* Loyal clientele will behave like fans and be more than happy to generate referrals at no cost to the business enterprise.

**Motivation**

If leaders want employees to perform well on a continuous basis, they should motivate employees on a continuous basis, via appreciation, respect, challenging assignments, participative management, an ethical environment, communication, feedback, training and development, money, etc. An employer-employee relationship is a business courtship or marriage, depending upon how the relationship is handled by both parties. Leadership is the art of achieving results through the efforts of other people who must be willing to perform the task(s) required of them — this willingness is usually the result of due motivation and job satisfaction. Congruence in the values of the organization, its top executives, and other employees leads to organizational effectiveness.
Job satisfaction and corporate welfare depend upon excellent leadership and the degree of motivation. Motivation may be characterized as a drive toward some goal(s) selected in preference to other possible goals. Job satisfaction results from motivation of employees who have been selected on the basis of merit and duly motivated via money, respect, fairness, training, challenging assignments, appreciation, participative management and other factors.

Every leader must serve the interests of the organization and all its stakeholders, so that the latter are geared toward working at their optimum level.
The problem with many leaders today is that they focus on short-term gains at the expense of medium- and long term gains, largely because the importance of quick results is overemphasized. Also, many leaders focus on increasing their share of the existing pie rather than on increasing the size of the overall pie and recognizing those who contributed to the same.

A smile, a pat on the back, and a free cheap lunch will only take you so far when motivating employees. Leaders should learn the true meaning and significance of teamwork, i.e. not just asking for cooperation from team members, but also being able and willing to share the rewards of teamwork with the team members.

As far as operating within an ethical environment is concerned, there is more to ethics than drafting the code of ethics for others to follow, drafting memos, sending e-mail messages and giving speeches accordingly. Leaders should lead by example and refrain from making false promises and unreasonable demands on others, or talking about the "green approach" as an exercise in public relations, instead of adopting a "green approach." Bullying in the workplace should not be tolerated and harassment of any kind should not be entertained.

**Communication**

Leaders should be able to communicate effectively with stakeholders and others in an attempt to exchange ideas with their goals in mind. Feedback should follow in order to ensure that the message was received correctly and understood. Sound communication builds relationships through an exchange of views, ideas, and opinions and promotes success in terms of the bottom line.

Leaders often spend more than 75 percent of the day listening and talking to stakeholders and others. Communication is maintained via conversations, interviews, meetings, conferences, training classes, written procedures, reports, memos, e-mail messages, texting, and other appropriate techniques, depending upon the situation at hand. To communicate effectively, one must understand the subject matter and one must tailor the presentation of the subject matter to suit the receiver of your message. Leaders should strive to understand and to be understood by their subordinates, peers, superiors and others by paying attention to words, expressions, images, body language, physical settings, and feelings of the speaker. Most problems between managers and others are centered around communication and often lead to loss of mutual trust and sincerity. Leaders must realize that they are dealing with human beings, who have feelings, different experiences, backgrounds, preconceived ideas, and beliefs. They must appreciate the status of the people involved and the nature of the information to be discussed.

Communication skills include listening, speaking, reading and writing and each must be consciously developed and delivered properly to the right person at the right time and place. Policies and procedures should be substantiated by reasons before being put into effect. Whenever you disagree with top management, make it known to them but not to your subordinates; otherwise, they may lose confidence in the business enterprise in question. The grapevine should be used advantageously by management instead of being allowed to adversely affect employee morale. False rumors should be disproved by facts.

**Training**

Training is a method of transferring knowledge and ability whereby the individual is taught what to do, how to do it, and why it should be done in a particular manner, with implications for the bottom line. Training may be effected on the job and via seminars and internal plus external courses.

People learn by listening, observing, and using their intellectual and emotional capacity in an attempt to help themselves and their employers. Trainees should be persuaded in favour of the training and tested to ensure that they meet the required standards. Trainees should be instilled with the desire to learn continuously and to promote goal congruence. Knowledge should be transferred gradually by a skilful instructor, in a friendly environment, with constant testing which includes case studies. The strengths of the trainees should be reinforced while their weaknesses are eliminated in a polite manner, without excessive emotion. Friendly competition helps stimulate transfer of the desired knowledge.

Lectures, classroom discussions, visual aids, on-the-job training, conferences, and correspondence courses are all useful methods of teaching and training employees. The specific method(s) of training that is/are adopted depend(s) on the goals of the training.

## Meetings

A large proportion of meetings waste a great deal of time and seem to be held for historical rather than practical reasons. Individuals can solve several crucial matters personally or upon informal consultation with others, although meetings do help develop the group feeling—a sense of belonging to the firm and its employees.

A stipulated quorum may be necessary to ensure that the meeting is valid.

*Functions of a Meeting*

1. To define the team/group/unit who will attend the meeting
2. To help revise and update important business matters
3. To help understand the group's interest and the individual's actual, plus potential contribution to the same
4. To help make group commitments in line with the firm's objectives
5. To help build and develop team spirit between those present at the meeting
6. To help individuals present at the meeting to ascertain their relative standings

Meetings may be held on a daily, weekly, or other basis.

*Prior to the Meeting*

(a) Define the objective(s)
(b) Prepare—people who must attend, agenda with appropriate headings—such as "for information," "for discussion," or "for decision"—to guide members present at the meetings. Papers attached to the agenda should be precise and well presented.
    The agenda should not be distributed much in advance of the meeting; otherwise, it may be misplaced. Items on the agenda should be arranged in order of priority. Mention the time at which the meeting is scheduled to begin and end; and if this exceeds ninety minutes, an

interval may be necessary.

*Election of a Chairperson*

This is essential to direct the course of the meeting. When two candidates have equal votes, the temporary chairperson has the *casting/decisive* vote.

**Drucker's View: The Corporation— A Symphony Orchestra?**

Peter Drucker is often considered to be the guru of management writers. Drucker believed that the modern "knowledge worker" owns the tools of production (i.e., his specific knowledge) and is therefore more mobile and flexible in approach and expectations than factory workers, who cannot carry the factory equipment wherever they go. Work is based on specialist knowledge. Knowledge workers are "associates" or "partners" who must be given a considerable amount of freedom and responsibility; otherwise, they will leave because they have their own tools of production, as discussed earlier. They are in favor of decentralization and a nonhierarchical structure as far as possible.

For instance, in a symphony orchestra, the first violin may be the most important in the orchestra, but the violinist in question is regarded as a colleague or associate rather than the boss or the superior of the other members of the orchestra. The other members of the orchestra play instruments that they specialize in. Similarly, in a hospital, a foot surgeon will be called upon to perform foot surgery. Even though a heart surgeon may be higher up on the pay scale than a foot surgeon, a heart surgeon cannot be expected to perform foot surgery because his/her knowledge is specific to the heart.

The manager/conductor of an orchestra faces the task of using the foregoing knowledge to ensure that the members of the orchestra operate in a synergistic approach, such that the whole performance is a true interpretation of the composer's score, of which each member is a genuine interpreter and performer within a team framework. What is required is a synchronized performance of the highest possible standards.

**Where Do We Go From Here?**

The past few years have witnessed several corporate scandals, adverse publicity and legal costs and there has been considerable talk of the importance of an ethical approach to business. The blind pursuit of profit has resulted in bribes, environmental problems, injured workers, unsafe products, closed plants, and so on. Ethics is concerned with "doing the right thing" but moral standards differ between individuals depending upon their upbringing, traditions, religion, social and economic situations, and other factors. Moreover, there is more to ethics than drafting and implementing codes of ethics for others to observe. Leaders should lead by example and refrain from adopting an approach which conflicts with ethical interests. Leaders should respect and care for all stakeholders: owners, employees, customers, suppliers, the community, etc., rather than stockholders alone. Making false promises and unreasonable demands on employees and others, preventing participative management, talking about the "green" approach as a public relations exercise, rather than adopting a "green" approach, is unacceptable. Ethics is conscience-based, knowledge-based and attitude-based, and not suited to individuals who have consistently demonstrated selfishness and greed. Business schools (and other schools) should adopt a practical rather than a mere philosophical approach to the teaching of ethics, while bearing in mind that ethics training can raise ethical IQs and help monitor behavior, but it is difficult to alter the basic nature of individuals such as Bernie Madoff, Conrad Black and Vincent Lacroix.

# BIBLIOGRAPHY

ULTIMATE Business Library   The Best Business Books Ever, Perseus, Bloomsbury, USA

Ambrecht, John           Estate Planning for the Family Business: The Non-Linear

                         Approach, USA, 2001

Belding, Shaun           Dealing with the Customer from Hell    Stoddart, Toronto, 2000

Blanchard, Ken,          Leadership Smarts, Honor Books, UK, 2004

Borden, Ladner,          It Begins with Service, PowerPoint Presentation, Canada, 2008.

Brown, D.R.,             The Living Franklin. Oak Brook, IL: Oakbrook Publishing

and Angee, A.N.          Group, Ltd., USA, 1975

Czepiel, John A.         "Managing Relationships with Customers: A Differentiation Philosophy of

                         Marketing, in Bowens, D.E., Chase, R.B. and Cummings, T.G.

                         Editions,1990

Drucker, Peter F.        The Daily Drucker, HarperCollins, USA, 2004

| | |
|---|---|
| Edersheim, Elizabeth | The Definitive Drucker, McGraw Hill, USA, 2007 |
| Fredrickson, J.W. | The Comprehensiveness of Strategic Decision Processes: Extension, observations, future directions. Academy of Management Journal, 27 (3), 445-457, (1984). |
| Green, Patrick | Family Wealth and Business Succession Planning, OSCPA, USA, 2007 |
| Handy, Charles | Inside Organizations, Penguin, London, 1990 |
| King, Patricia | Never Work for a Jerk! Dorset Press, USA, 1987 |
| Kuratko, D. F. | Strategic Choices. Journal of Small Business Management 31 (2), 38-50, (1993). |
| Leach, P | Family Business, Thomson Carswell, Canada, 2003 |
| Ball, Bruce | |
| Duncan, Garry | |
| Leland, K., and Bailey, K. | Customer Service for Dummies, Foster City, USA, 1995: |
| Lencioni, Patrick | The Five Dysfunctions of a Team - *A Leadership Fable*, Jossey-Bass, USA, 2002 |
| Lynch, A., | *All in the Family Inc.*, Macmillan, Canada, 2001. DG Books Worldwide, Inc. |
| Lyles, M. A., Baird, J. S., | Formalized planning in small business: Increasing |
| Orris, J. B., | Strategic Choices, Butler University Library, USA, 1994. |
| McCormack, Mark | Staying Street Smart in the Internet Age, Viking Penguin, New York, 2000. |
| *Miller, Danny and* | *Managing for the Long Run: Lessons in Competitive Advantage* |

| | |
|---|---|
| *Miller, Isabelle* | *from Great Family Businesses*, Harvard Business School Press and McGraw Hill, USA, 2005 |
| Moorhead, G. and Griffin, R.W | Organizational Behavior. 4th ed. Boston, MA: Houghton-Mifflin Company, 1995. |
| Pinto, Maxwell | Leadership: Flirting with Disaster!, Amazon.com, USA, 2011. |
| Pinto, Maxwell | Management: Tidbits for the New Millennium, Amazon.com, USA, 2011 |
| Pinto, Maxwell | The Management Syndrome: How to Deal with It!, Amazon.com, USA, 2011 |
| Pinto, Maxwell | Leadership and Ethics: Major Ingredients of the Business Recipe, Amazon.com, USA, 2011 |
| Porter, M. E. | Competitive Strategy for Analyzing Industries and Competitors, The Free Press, New York, 1980. |
| Reichheld, Fred, | "The One Number You Need to Grow," Harvard Business Review, December 2003. |
| Savage, Jack | The Everything Home Based Business Book, Adams Media Corporation, Massachusetts, USA, 2000. |
| Saxby, David | Measure-X, a Phoenix, Ariz.-based measurement, training and recognition company that specializes in customer service and sales skills training for utilities. www.measure-x.com. |
| Schwass, Joachim | Wise Growth Strategies in Leading Family Businesses, |

Palgrave Macmillan, USA, 2005

| | |
|---|---|
| Trunk, Penelope | Brazen Careerist – The New Rules for Success, Warner Business Books, New York, 2007 |
| Wees, Aida Van | Enhancing the Value of the Family Owned Business, The Legal Outsourcing Network, Canada, 2008 |
| Weigl, Corina McGowan, Luanna | Succession Planning Toolkit for Business Owners, The Canadian Institute of Chartered Accountants, Canada, 2006. |
| Wright, P., Kroll, M. J., and Parnell, J. | Strategic Management: Concepts and Cases. 3rd Ed. Englewood Cliffs, NJ: Prentice Hall, Inc., (1996). |

## Articles by:

1. Allen R. DeCotiis, Ph.D., Chairman and Chief Executive Officer, Phoenix Marketing International and Paul Singer, Client Partner, Scient, Inc. The Value of the Ideal Customer Experience, ServiceSat.com. Phoenix Marketing International, Fall 2001, study consists of almost 20,000 respondents.

2. Anderson, Eugene W. and Claes Fornell (1994), "A Customer Satisfaction Research Prospectus," in *Service Quality: New Directions in Theory and Practice*, R. T. Rust and R. L. Oliver, eds. Thousand Oaks, CA: Sage Publications, Inc., 241-268.

3. Bellenger, Danny N., Earle Steinberg, and Wilbur Stanton (1976), "The Congruence of Store Image and Self Image: As It Relates to Store Loyalty," *Journal of Retailing*, 52 (Spring), 17-32.

4. Berry, Leonard L. (1983), "Relationship Marketing," in *Emerging Perspectives on Services Marketing*,

5. L. L. Berry, G. L. Shostack, and G. D. Upah, eds. Chicago, IL: American Marketing Association, 25-28. Bowen, John (1990), "Development of a Taxonomy of Services to Gain Strategic

6. Relationship Marketing," in *1989 AMA Winter Educators' Conference: Marketing Theory and Practice*, T. L. Childers, R. P. Bagozzi, et al., eds. Chicago, IL: AMA, 216-220. Marketing Insights," *Journal of the Academy of Marketing Science*, 18 (Winter), 43-49.

7. Crosby, Lawrence A., Kenneth Evans, and Deborah Cowles (1990), "Relationship Quality in Services Selling: An Interpersonal Influence Perspective," *Journal of Marketing*, 54 (July), 68-81.

8. Cronin, J. Joseph, Jr. and Steven A. Taylor (1992), "Measuring Service Quality: A Re-examination and Extension," *Journal of Marketing*, 56 (July), 55-68.

9. Czepiel, John A. and Robert Gilmore (1987), "Exploring the Concept of Loyalty in Services," in *The Services Marketing Challenge: Integrating for Competitive Advantage*, J. A. Czepiel, C. A. Congram, and J. Shanahan, eds. Chicago, IL: AMA, 91-94.

10. Day, George S. (1971), "A Two-Dimensional Concept of Brand Loyalty," *Journal of Advertising Research*, 9 (September), 29-36. Dick, Alan S. and Kunal Basu (1994), "Customer Loyalty: Toward an Integrated Conceptual Framework," *Journal of the Academy of Marketing Science*, 22 (Spring), 99-113.

11. Dwyer, F. Robert, Paul H. Schurr, and Sejo Oh (1987), "Developing Buyer-Seller Relationships," *Journal of Marketing*, 51 (April), 11-27. Fornell, Claes (1992), "A National Customer Satisfaction Barometer: The Swedish Experience," *Journal of Marketing*, 56 (January), 6-21.

12. Guiltinan, Joseph P. (1989), "A Classification of Switching Costs with Implications for

Hamm, B.A., (2003). Want a company you can be truly proud of? Try a business ethics program. Retrieved Aug. 17, 2007 from http://www.compassolutions.biz/id25.htm/

13. Jacoby, Jacob and Robert W. Chestnut (1978), *Brand Loyalty: Measurement and Management*, New York, NY: John Wiley and Sons, Inc.

14. Jain, Arun K., Christian Pinson, and Naresh K. Malhotra (1987), "Customer Loyalty as a Construct in the Marketing of Banking Services," *International Journal of Bank Marketing*, 5 (3), 49-72.

15. James Gehrke, Steps for Ethical Leadership in Today's Organizations http://ezinearticles.com/?6-Steps-for-Ethical-Leadership-in-Todays-Organizationsandid=934392

16. Jarvis, Lance P. and James B. Wilcox (1976), "Repeat Purchasing Behavior and Attitudinal Brand Loyalty: Additional Evidence," in *Marketing: 1776-1976 and Beyond*, K. L. Bernhardt, ed. Chicago, IL: American Marketing Association, 151-152.

17. Johnson, Michael P. (1982), "Social and Cognitive Features of the Dissolution of Commitment to Relationships," in *Personal Relationships, Volume 4: Dissolving Personal Relationships*, Vol. 4, S. Duck, eds. New York: Academic Press, 51-73.

18. Lee, Barrett A. and Carol A. Zeiss (1980), "Behavioral Commitment to the Role of Sport Consumer: An Exploratory Analysis," *Sociology and Social Research*, 64 (April), 405-419.

19. Lincoln, Yvonna S. and Egon G. Guba (1985), *Naturalistic Inquiry*, Newbury Park, CA: Sage Publications, 187-220.

20. Murray, Keith B. (1991), "A Test of Services Marketing Theory: Consumer Information Acquisition Activities," *Journal of Marketing*, 55 (January), 10-25.

21. Oliva, Terence A., Richard L. Oliver, and Ian C. MacMillan (1992), "A Catastrophe Model for Developing Service Satisfaction Strategies," *Journal of Marketing*, 56 (July), 83-95.

22. Oliver, Richard L. and Gerald Linda (1981), "Effect of Satisfaction and Its Antecedents on Consumer Preference and Intention," in *Advances in Consumer Research*, Vol. 8, K. B. Monroe, ed. Ann Arbor, MI: Association for Consumer Research, 88-93.

23. Ostrowski, Peter L., Terrence O'Brien, and Geoffrey Gordon (1993), "Service Quality and Customer Loyalty in the Commercial Airline Industry," *Journal of Travel Research*, 32 (Fall), 16-24.

24. Parasuraman, A., Valarie A. Zeithaml, and Leonard L. Berry (1985), "A Conceptual Model of Service Quality and Its Implications for Future Research," *Journal of Marketing*, 49 (Fall), 41-50.

25. Pritchard, Mark P. (1991), "Development of the Psychological Commitment Instrument (PCI) for Measuring Travel Service Loyalty," doctoral dissertation, University of Oregon. 29.

26. Reichheld, Frederick F. (1993), "Loyalty-Based Management," *Harvard Business Review*, 71 (March-April), 64-73.

27. Reynolds, Fred D., William R. Darden, and Warren S. Martin (1975), "Developing an Image of the Store-Loyal Customer: A Life-Style Analysis to Probe a Neglected Market," *Journal of Retailing*, 50 (Winter), 73-84.

28. Snyder, Don R. (1986), "Service Loyalty and Its Measurement: A Preliminary Investigation," in *Creativity in Service Marketing: What's New, What Works, What's Developing*, M. Venkatesan, D. M. Schmalensee, and C. Marshall, eds. Chicago, IL: AMA, 44-48.Surprenant,

29. Carol F. and Michael R. Solomon (1987), "Predictability and Personalization in the Service Encounter," *Journal of Marketing*, 51 (April), 86-96.

30. Zeithaml, Valarie A. (1981), "How Consumer Evaluation Processes Differ Between Goods and Services," in *Marketing of Services*, J. H. Donnelly and W. R. George, eds. Chicago, IL: American Marketing Association, 186-190.

31. Zeithaml, Valarie A., Leonard L. Berry, and A. Parasuraman (1996), "The Behavioral Consequences of Service Quality," *Journal of Marketing*, 60 (August), (forthcoming).

32. Marcus Z. Cox, Stephen F., Alicia B. Gresham and Stephen F. Austin State University. The Role of Customer Service in Small Business Strategic Planning

33. BBC News, June 20, 2002, Crowe 'deserved to be exposed'

http://news.bbc.co.uk/2/hi/entertainment/2055286.stm

34. BBC News, November 28, 2005, Crowe Jokes about Phone Incident

http://news.bbc.co.uk/2/hi/entertainment/4477178.stm

35. People, June 24, 2002, Judge Tosses Out Crowe Plotters' Case

By Stephen M. Silverman

ttp://www.people.com/people/article/0,,624140,00.html

36. People Magazine, June 9, 2005, Russell Crowe Sorry for 'Shameful' Conduct

By Stephen M. Silverman

http://www.people.com/people/article/0,,1070328,00.html

37. People Magazine, November 28, 2005   Russell Crowe Mocks Phone-Throwing Incident

http://www.people.com/people/article/0,,1134863,00.html

38. People Magazine, November 3, 2006   Russell Crowe Calls Phone-Toss Overplayed

By Stephen M. Silverman

http://www.people.com/people/article/0,,1554602,00.html

39. The Superficial, November 18, 2005 Russell Crowe finally Settles Phone Incident

http://www.thesuperficial.com/archives/2005/11/18/russel_crowe_gets_sentenced.html

40. CNN June 6, 2005, Russell Crowe Appears in Court - Actor arrested on charges related to phone-throwing incident

http://www.cnn.com/2005/SHOWBIZ/Movies/06/06/crowe.arrest/

41. The Independent, November 7, 2008, Russell Crowe: "Angry? Me? Never"

By Gill Pringle

http://www.independent.co.uk/arts-entertainment/films/features/russell-crowe-angry-me-never-997593.ht

42. American Psychology Association Controlling Anger before it Controls You

http://www.apa.org/topics/controlanger.html

American Psychological Association, Washington, DC © 2006 http://www.angerclassonline.com

43. Customer Experience Management Best Practices - Profitable Growth through Customer Centricity © 2005 Satmetrix Systems, Inc.

http://www.satmetrix.com/satmetrix/pdfs/sm-wp-CEM-best-practices.pdf

44. Wikipedia http://en.wikipedia.org/wiki/Naomi_Campbell

45. Wikipedia http://en.wikipedia.org/wiki/Russell_Crowe

46. Wikipedia http://en.wikipedia.org/wiki/The_Insider_(film)

http://www.cwanswers.com/8921/naomi_campbell

47. Quinn, R. (2005). Moments of greatness: Entering the fundamental state of leadership. Harvard Business Review, July - August 2005. 75-83.

48. Trevino, L., and Nelson, K., (2005). Corporate social responsibility and managerial ethics. Hoboken, NJ: John Wiley and Sons, Inc.

Article Source: http://EzineArticles.com/?expert=James_Gehrke

49. Bernard Madoff avoids jail

Ed Pilkington in New York

guardian.co.uk, Monday 12 January 2009 19.40 GMT

Article history

http://www.guardian.co.uk/business/2009/jan/13/madoff-bail-decision

50. In Business - Trust is Essential

By Ben Carlsen

http://ezinearticles.com/?In-Business---Trust-is-Essentialandid=1795711

Copyright © 2008, Dr. Ben A. Carlsen, MBA. All Rights Reserved Worldwide for all Additional information can be obtained at http://drben.info

Article Source: http://EzineArticles.com/?expert=Ben_Carlsen

51. How to Tackle Human Rights Issues at Work?

By Sarah Jose

http://ezinearticles.com/?How-to-Tackle-Human-Rights-Issues-at-Work?andid=1853742

Article Source: http://EzineArticles.com/?expert=Sarah_Jose

52. Ethics in the Workplace

By Natalie Rhoden

http://ezinearticles.com/?Ethics-in-the-Workplaceandid=1648959

53. Employees Sometimes Lack Ethics

By Cash Miller ☆

http://ezinearticles.com/?Employees-Sometimes-Lack-Ethicsandid=1639057

Article Source: http://EzineArticles.com/?expert=Cash_Miller

54. Ethical Practices - You Are What You Believe

By Janet B

http://ezinearticles.com/?Ethical-Practices---You-Are-What-You-Believeandid=1704109

© Janet L. Burgar, November 2008

Article Source: http://EzineArticles.com/?expert=Janet_B

55. Is Corporate Ethics Beneficial to the Bottom Line?

By Nathan Warren

http://ezinearticles.com/?Is-Corporate-Ethics-Beneficial-to-the-Bottom-Line?andid=1574455

Nathan Warren owns and operates http://www.ethiceducation.com - Ethics Education

Article Source: http://EzineArticles.com/?expert=Nathan_Warren

56. Green Ethics For Green Businesses

By Michael Richmond

http://ezinearticles.com/?Green-Ethics-For-Green-Businessesandid=1651136

http://EzineArticles.com/?expert=Michael_Richmond

57. Discrimination in the Workplace

By Robert Coffen

http://ezinearticles.com/?Discrimination-in-the-Workplaceandid=1696842

Article Source: http://EzineArticles.com/?expert=Robert_Coffen

58. Total Leadership - Ethical Behavior Is Essential

How did we ever get from George Washington's "I cannot tell a lie" to "I refuse to testify?"The Fifth Amendment...

by Patricia Wallington

http://www.cio.com/article/31779/Total_Leadership_Ethical_Behaviour_Is_Essential?page=3

59. The Color Of Ethics Is Gray-Part One

By Jim Blasingame BRAINTRUST April 15, 2003
http://www.smallbusinessadvocate.com/small-business-articles/the-color-of-ethics-is-gray-part-one-236

60. The Color Of Ethics Is Gray- Part Two

By Jim Blasingame BRAINTRUST April 15, 2003
http://www.smallbusinessadvocate.com/small-business-articles/the-color-of-ethics-is-gray-part-two-237
Complete Guide to Ethics Management: An Ethics Toolkit for Managers
Written by Carter McNamara, MBA, PhD, Authenticity Consulting, LLC. Copyright 1997-2008.
http://www.managementhelp.org/ethics/ethxgde.htm on the Web.)

61. $200m is more than an 'error'

Kelly McParland, National Post  Published: Tuesday, September 22, 2009

http://www.nationalpost.com/news/story.html?id=2017800

Peter J. Thompson/National Post

62. Pictures related to garbage strike in Toronto taken from

http://www.larrycornies.com/2009/07/toronto-mayor-david-miller-and-the-macleans-cover/
http://www2.macleans.ca/tag/david-miller/

www.ingramcontent.com/pod-product-compliance
Lightning Source LLC
Chambersburg PA
CBHW080845170526
45158CB00009B/2632